INTRODUCING CHINCHILLAS

WHAT IS A CHINCHILLA?

The chinchilla's natural habitat is high in the Andes of Bolivia, Peru, Chile, and Argentina. Classified as members of the order Rodentia, chinchillas are small rodents related to squirrels, guinea pigs, mice, hamsters, and gerbils. Chinchillas are the most expensive of all rodents in the world because their soft fur is the most sought-after of all skins used in making fur garments.

The two species of chinchillas, *Chinchilla brevicaudata* and *Chinchilla lanigera*, are outwardly almost indistinguishable. Both species have long hind limbs, short forelimbs, four toes, and flexible digits. *C. brevicaudata* presents a stockier appearance than *C. lanigera*. It has a thicker neck and shoulders, shorter ears, and a flatter nose than *C. lanigera*. It is heavily furred with light gray hair often tinged with a

The chinchilla is best known for its beautiful, luxuriant fur. Chinchillas are native to the Andes Mountains in South America.

yellowish hue. *C. lanigera* has a sleeker look because of its narrower neck and shoulders and somewhat more pointed face and elongated ears. The fur is very silky, usually medium to dark gray with a bright bluish cast. Only *C. lanigera* is commonly available.

Similar to other rodents such as beavers, hamsters, and guinea pigs, chinchillas have two continuously growing incisor teeth in the upper jaw and two in the lower jaw. They are nocturnal animals, being active mostly at dusk and at night. During daylight hours in the wild, they

Chinchillas are rodents. As such they have continuously growing incisor teeth, which must be kept in trim to prevent dental problems. POPpups™, manufactured by the Nylabone Corporation, are an excellent means of keeping your chinchilla's teeth to the proper length.

A young black male chinchilla and its charcoal father.

sleep in dark hiding places such as holes and crevices. As the sun goes down they begin to search for food.

What sets chinchillas apart from the rest of the rodents is their fur. It is so silky, dense, light, and soft that it is virtually unmatched by any other fur-bearing animal. Each hair grows in an agouti pattern of three colored bands: the lower zone (undercoat), the band, and the veil (clouding). Special guard hairs

Chinchillas are nocturnal animals, which means that they are most active at night.

protrude a few tenths of an inch (several millimeters) beyond the undercoat of the fur and provide elasticity to a mature pelt. The abdominal fur usually does not have the agouti markings but instead is a solid patch of white to light gray.

Both species were originally brought to the United States to be bred as fur producers. Since *C. lanigera* adapted better to captivity and reproduced better, *C. brevicaudata* was eventually

specimens became the first chinchillas offered as commercial pets. Today most pets on the market have been bred for just that purpose.

C. brevicaudata and *C. lanigera* are now mostly extinct in their original range. Protected by their governments, chinchillas cannot legally be hunted or trapped, but the hungry natives still eat them (and guinea pigs, too). The wild chinchilla population is on the U.S. Endangered Species list.

A brown velvet male. The chinchilla's fur is so soft and silky that it is virtually unmatched by any other furred mammal.

dropped from most fur-farming programs. Therefore, it is generally assumed that most of the animals in the United States are *C. lanigera* descendants. Culls and other poor fur

CHAPMAN AND CHINCHILLAS

South American natives had been fashioning chinchilla fur into warm, lightweight garments for hundreds of years. When Spanish explorers arrived on the continent

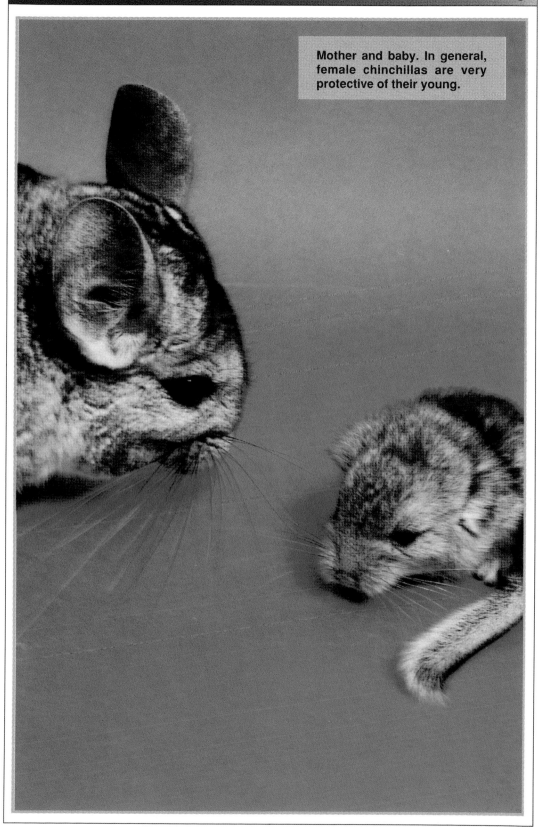

Mother and baby. In general, female chinchillas are very protective of their young.

in the 1500's, they collected the pelts for their return trips. The limited amount of fur was soon used to trim royal robes and gowns.

Over the years, several attempts were made to bring chinchillas down from the mountains to establish breeding herds. Unfortunately, the animals never

M.F. Chapman, a mining engineer from California, was working in Chile in 1918. A native entered Chapman's camp to sell a chinchilla he had captured. Chapman purchased the animal as a pet and took a real liking to it. Subsequently, he envisioned raising a whole herd of chinchillas.

Chinchillas are curious about their environment and will investigate new objects by sniffing or pawing at them.

survived the trip. Finally, one group did survive the descent and the first chinchilla farm was established near San Antonio de los Cobre, Argentina. The 36 animals died in captivity, though, and the venture failed.

Even though Chapman knew of the previous unsuccessful attempts with chinchillas, he was determined to establish his own herd. He applied to the Chilean government for permission to capture and

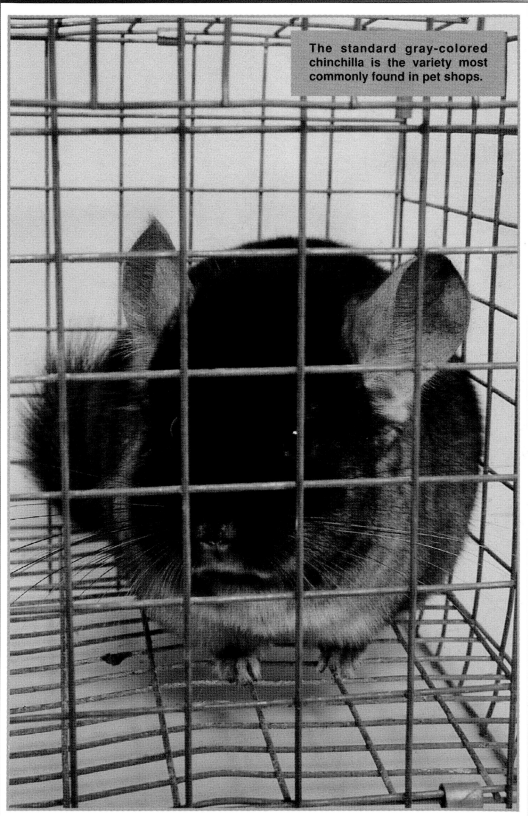

The standard gray-colored chinchilla is the variety most commonly found in pet shops.

transport several animals to the United States. By this time, chinchillas were already close to extinction as a result of excessive trapping.

Understandably, the Chilean government was reluctant to grant trapping privileges, much less allow transport out of the country. But Chapman persisted, and eventually the government relented.

Chapman and a trapping party of 23 men traversed the mountains to catch as many chinchillas as possible. The population was so sparse that only 11 acceptable specimens were captured in three years.

Chapman theorized that other trappers had failed to give the chinchillas enough time to acclimate themselves to the changing environment during the descent. Following his theory, the 12,000-foot trip down the mountain was gradually completed over a period of 12 months. The cages were cooled with blocks of ice and shaded from direct sunlight. The slow descent and painstaking care paid off, because all 11 chinchillas survived.

The animals were then boarded on a ship to complete their journey to the United States. Due to Chapman's continued caution, the chinchillas not only survived but multiplied! One kit was born during the trip.

On his ranch in California, Chapman experimented with housing and feeding. In the wild, chinchillas feed on seeds, grasses, and yareta, a South American plant. On the trip down the mountain Chapman gathered local vegetation to feed the herd. Away from South America, he tried to duplicate the diet as closely as possible. Initially the chinchillas had some difficulty, but through experimentation Chapman developed a sound feeding program and suitable living quarters. As his animals thrived and multiplied, he offered them for sale. Since they were so rare, one pair sold for $3200.

More chinchilla ranches developed throughout the United States, and by the middle 1960's thousands of animals were available. Eventually, some chinchillas found their way into the pet market. Today more and more chinchillas are being offered as pets, but most animals are still raised for their fine pelts, especially in Europe.

CHINCHILLAS AS PETS

When purchasing any pet, both the advantages and disadvantages must be considered. For any pet to thrive, not merely survive, it requires a home to which it is well suited.

Chinchillas are ideal pets in homes that cannot accommodate larger domestic pets. No apartment is too small to house a chinchilla cage. The animals' small size, cleanliness, hardiness, and ease of care make them ideal indoor pets. They are a long-lasting source of entertainment, yet they can be kept safely out of harm's way.

Chinchillas pose no serious threat to children, strangers, or

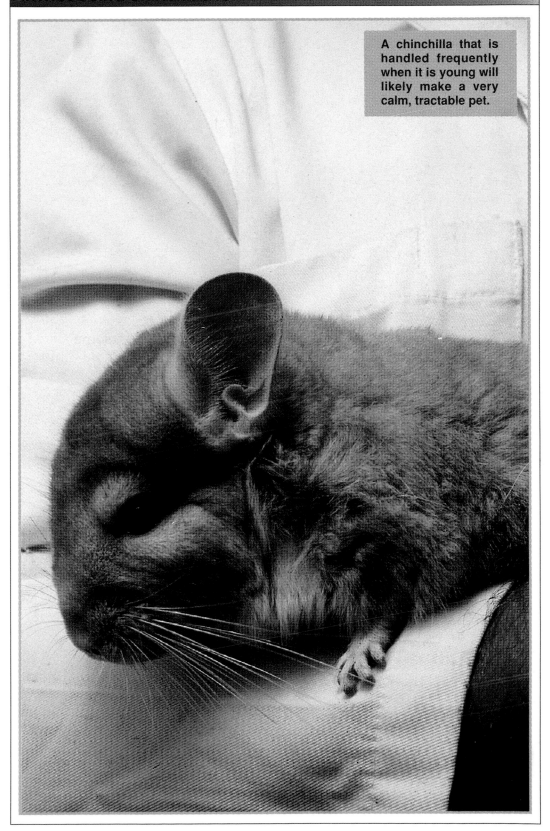

A chinchilla that is handled frequently when it is young will likely make a very calm, tractable pet.

Chinchillas make good pets. They are small, quiet, and clean.

other animals, since they are not aggressive by nature. They may occasionally nip, but even a "true" bite is seldom severe.

Chinchillas are available in pet shops. They can be purchased for a reasonable price, including all the necessary equipment and supplies. Chinchillas require little maintenance, and the subsequent expenses are minimal. Food and water need to be freshened daily, and the cage and accessories need routine cleaning. Since they are vegetarians, their diet of pellets and hay is simple, inexpensive, and available all year. Chinchillas are sensitive to even slight dietary changes, so great care must be taken in offering treats.

Being nocturnal animals, chinchillas must be afforded a quiet and dark place to rest during the day. They are not the pet of choice for owners who want a daytime companion. No rodent is.

Chinchillas can be left alone for a couple of days with the proper provisions, but if a more extended absence is anticipated, a reliable person needs to be available to replenish the food and water at least every other day. Of course, a chinchilla's cage is easily transportable to another location to receive care. Just be sure to guard against sudden extreme or extended changes in temperature during transport.

Most pets adapt to handling, but further training takes some time. Advanced training is limited to simple tricks, and requires patience and persistence to bring about the desired results. Animals of a young age are more receptive to both taming and training.

Chinchillas seem to flourish better in pairs, However, the pair must be a male-female match. Housing two like animals will result in savage fighting. Even mated pairs have been known to have spats, so the living quarters must be roomy enough to provide hiding space to keep fighting to a minimum. Bear in mind that under the right conditions, chinchillas breed readily. If you don't want chinchilla progeny, then it is best to get just one pet.

Chinchillas never need to be taken outside for a walk like dogs. On the other hand, not many chinchillas have been housebroken. If you allow your pet to roam the house, chinchilla droppings and fur (yes, chinchillas do shed) will be found in every spot your pal has visited. Fortunately, the droppings are small, firm, and odorless. Both hair and droppings are easily swept away or vacuumed up.

Unlike cats and dogs, chinchillas should not be permitted to explore a home without supervision. Left unattended, the animals are apt to chew electrical cords and furniture. If you don't keep track of just where you pet is at all times, you may be hard pressed to find him. Chinchillas can fit into the most surprising places! They are fast runners and high jumpers, so it might take some ingenuity on your part to trap a chinchilla that doesn't want to be caught.

Usually dogs and cats take well to chinchillas, but you can never be sure how an animal is going to react. Be prepared to keep any other pets strictly supervised until you are sure that they pose no threat to your chinchillas. Some exotic animals, like snakes and ferrets, are natural enemies and must never be put into contact with chinchillas.

Unlike many other indoor pets, chinchillas do not emit strong odors. They can be kept without being offensive to sensitive human noses. (However, there may be those few noses that experience an allergic reaction to them.) Although chinchillas may occasionally make grunting or chirping noises, the sound is barely audible and not a nuisance to neighbors.

Chinchillas are very clean animals. Presumably because their fur is so dense, they do not harbor parasites such as fleas and ticks. To keep the fur at its optimum, chinchillas need regular combing and a "bath" in special sand.

All in all, chinchillas are soft, playful, inquisitive balls of fur that provide years of fun and puppy-like frolic. Being unusual pets, they attract lots of attention to both themselves and their owners.

When fully grown, a chinchilla measures about 12 inches in length. In general, females are usually larger than males.

When selecting a chinchilla, look for one that is bright eyed and alert.

THE PET CHINCHILLA

SELECTION

In some areas, locating a source for buying a chinchilla may pose a challenge. The best place to start looking is in your local pet shop. Most shops will stock only a pet or two, and some never display them at all. However, most shop owners know how to obtain the animals, and some may even be able to fill special requests regarding age and color.

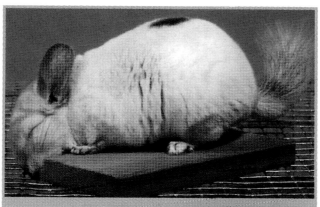

This chinchilla is gnawing on a piece of wood. It would be safer and healthier to provide it with a chew device of the kind found in pet shops. Your pet shop dealer can advise you what products are suitable for chinchillas.

Choose a dealer with a long-standing record of supplying good stock. He won't purposely sell a poor specimen that may mar his high standing. Choose a store with clean, neat cages and well stocked inventories. These dealers care about their animals and will probably have all the accessories you need to care for your chinchilla. If the animals are well-fed and well-housed, they are more likely to be healthy specimens. Seek out well-informed employees, because they are the ones upon whom you will rely for sound advice.

Observe the chinchilla for a while. It should be alert and bright-eyed. Watery discharge from the nose and eyes indicates a health problem. The fur should be sleek and well-groomed, not wet or knotted. Matted hair around the nose and on the forelimbs means that the animal has been wiping a runny discharge from its nose.

The chinchilla should move easily and quickly about its cage. An animal that moves with difficulty, or has labored breathing, is best avoided.

Before purchasing it, always hold a chinchilla to evaluate its temperament and more closely examine its physical condition. Approach the cage slowly. Speak softly and calmly to the animal so as not to alarm it. Sudden movements, especially those that produce shadows, are frightening to a chinchilla. Open the cage door and allow the animal a few moments to become acquainted with you. Let it sniff at your hand, "nibble" at your fingers and jewelry, and tug at your sleeves. Very few chinchillas bite hard except in self-defense.

Lift the chinchilla and support its weight with both of your hands. Never grab it by the fur — you will only be left with a handful of hair because one of the defense mechanisms of a chinchilla is its ability to release its fur if caught.

dense fur gives the impression of a much larger size. Regardless of size, the chinchilla should feel solid with no protruding bones. The ears should be clean and free of scabs. Examine the teeth. They should be creamy yellow in color, never white. The top teeth should overlap the bottom ones, and both sets should be fairly straight across. Tooth abnormalities are a serious problem for chinchillas. Such

The domestic chinchilla is known scientifically as *Chinchilla lanigera*.

The chinchilla may struggle at first, but a good pet will not become unduly frantic or frightened. When the animal realizes that you intend it no harm, it should settle down and may even become relaxed.

You may be surprised to realize just how small the animal really is, because its

animals must be avoided by pet owners.

Place the chinchilla back in its cage. It may scamper away, but it will probably return to the cage door for more attention. Offer it a treat of a sunflower seed or a raisin. The chinchilla should finish the treat quickly without drooling.

This chinchilla is attempting to climb over its owner's hand. Chinchillas are remarkably agile little animals.

Young animals are more receptive to taming. However, do not purchase a chinchilla until it has been away from its mother for at least one week and is eating well. Weaning is stressful for a youngster. Coupled with being removed from its mother and placed in unfamiliar surroundings, weaning may prove to be too much for a chinchilla, resulting in sickness or even death.

If you want a pet for immediate breeding purposes, the chinchilla should be no less than eight months old. If buying a breeding pair, choose a couple that has been living together and is of proven compatibility. Remember never to house two animals of like sex together.

Chinchilla droppings are a good indicator of fitness. Look at the bottom of the cage and notice the pellets. They should be dark brown, firm, slightly moist, oblong, and of a relatively uniform size. If the droppings are discolored, or in any other way obviously differ from the description, the chinchilla may be suffering from some ailment.

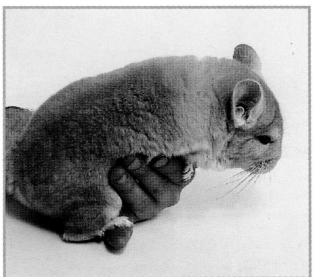
In gray chinchillas, the intensity of color can vary dramatically from one individual to another.

Both sexes of chinchillas make wonderful pets. Neither the male nor the female is noticeably calmer, more attractive, or more lovable. Each individual chinchilla has its own personality, and this is the attribute on which a pet should be judged.

COLORS

The original and most prevalent color of chinchillas is gray, ranging from pale gray to almost black. This is known as the "standard" chinchilla. As early as the 1940's, color mutations began showing up on the ranches. The most common color variations are white, beige, and black.

WHITE: Born on a ranch in North Carolina, the first white male arrived in 1955. This was not a true albino, which would have pink ears and reddish pink eyes. Rather, the offspring of this white, known as Wilson Whites, have black-tipped ears and black eyes.

Nowadays, white chinchillas are less expensive than good quality standards. Their pelts are not highly regarded in the fur trade because they are

Young children must be supervised when they handle a chinchilla. If a chinchilla is held in a clumsy manner, it may bite.

White chinchilla. This color variety first appeared on a ranch in North Carolina in 1955.

indistinguishable from white rabbit pelts. A pure white chinchilla pelt is uniformly white. It does not display the tri-colored agouti hair pattern of normal chinchilla fur.

The mating of a white and a standard produces 50% whites and 50% standards in the first generation. The white offspring may be of several varieties, however. They may be pure white or white with black guard hairs, or the progeny may be silver white or platinum white. Both of these latter types display the common agouti fur pattern once again. Silver chinchillas have a silver-gray undercoat, a white band, and a silver-gray veil. Platinum chinchillas have a light blue undercoat, a bluish white band, and a bluish clouding. Mosaics, or pieds, may also occur. The veil is not uniform, but is arranged in patches of gray or silver.

Mating two whites produces descendants that are pure white. However, these animals have an inherent lethal genetic factor. Mating whites to standards or off-colored chinchillas is important in the development of new color mutations.

BEIGE: In 1955, a beige female was born on a ranch in Oregon. The descendants became known as Crown of Sunset Beiges and were quite popular.

Light beige (pearl), and medium to dark beiges (pastel), result from the mating of a beige buck and a clear-blue standard female. Crossing beige with white produces cream-colored offspring referred to as Rose or Apricot.

Mating beige and beige gives either dark beige or rose animals. If existing genetic features are dominant, other characteristics may occur.

BLACK: Black mutations developed in 1956. Known as Black Velvets, these animals have a black undercoat, a narrow gray-white band, and a jet-black veil.

Mating a black chinchilla with clear-colored standards produced the Blue Black Velvet. Matings of black bucks with females of other mutations resulted in Sapphire Velvets, Pastel Velvets, and Brown Velvets.

New mutations, such as the Sullivan Violet, are still appearing on ranches due to continued crossbreeding. These mutants are far too rare and valuable to be offered for sale as pets.

SEXING

Check a chinchilla's sex yourself if you are matching up pairs. Classifying newborns can be difficult, and sometimes even experienced ranchers have made incorrect determinations.

An initial observation may confuse a novice because the female's urethral cone may be mistaken for a penis. If you have one of each sex for comparison, sexing is made easier. In mature males there is a considerable separation, about 1/2 inch (1 to 1.5 cm), between the anus and penis. In females the urethral cone is directly next to the anus. The vaginal opening is sometimes visible as a horizontal slit between the urethral cone and anus. When the female comes into estrus, or "heat," the vagina opens up and is more obvious. The female chinchilla has six nipples, three along each side of her abdomen.

Males and females also have different body types and can be distinguished (by an experienced eye) on that basis. Males are generally smaller than females, with a wider and more massive head. Females are usually larger than males, though with a more compact appearance.

Females have one more identifying characteristic. As a defensive maneuver, females rise up on their hind legs, aim their clitoris at an intruder, and direct a spray of urine at the eyes.

HANDLING

Because a chinchilla may bite or shed fur if cornered and frightened, speak softly to yours before you touch it. A calm voice seems to have a soothing effect. When your pet is still, place one hand behind it (chinchillas can scamper backward with amazing speed) and slide your free hand under its abdomen. You may grasp the tail to help still the chinchilla, but hold it as close to the root as possible to prevent breakage. Now slowly raise the animal, always supporting its full weight. Never leave a chinchilla dangling.

The chinchilla can be placed against your chest with its head looking over your shoulder and one hand supporting its rump in much the same way that you would cradle a baby. You can also tip the chinchilla to a reclining position in which the chinchilla lies belly up, with one hand behind its back and the other hand under its hindquarters.

CAGES AND ACCESSORIES

SELECTION: Before bringing your new pet home, have the cage and all the equipment prepared for its arrival. The pet dealer will probably place the chinchilla in a box for transport; having the cage ready and waiting means less time spent in the box. Advance preparation eases the chinchilla's transition and helps him to feel comfortable.

Each adult chinchilla requires its own cage; like-sexed adults refuse to live peacefully together. A male-female pair should share the same cage for breeding purposes, but only after a careful introduction. There should be ample room in the cage for a chinchilla to run about and to stand erect on its hind legs. Therefore, choose the largest cage you can afford and comfortably accommodate. Experienced breeders recommend the following dimensions: 24 inches wide, 24 inches deep, and 22 inches high. The minimum suitable size is 20 x 20 x 26 inches. Anything smaller is too confining and will dampen a chinchilla's lively nature.

Stainless steel wire mesh, thick enough to withstand a chinchilla's chewing, is preferred. The wire is easy to clean and resists corrosion. Chicken wire is inappropriate because it is thin and rusts easily. Cages with plastic-coated bars may appear easy to maintain, but a chinchilla will readily chew the coating and make a mess in the process. Wooden cages are also hungrily gnawed, and the wood absorbs urine and harbors parasites.

Inspect the cage closely before buying it. Be sure there are no protruding wires or sharp corners. If you plan to breed chinchillas, the openings in the mesh should be no larger than 1 inch so that baby chinchillas cannot escape.

and food to pass through to a metal sheet below. This drop pan is lined with litter and is simply slid out for cleaning without disturbing your pet. This cage style promotes good health, because it keeps soiled food from the chinchilla's reach and allows you to monitor the animal's droppings for signs of illness.

Have the cage set up before you bring your chinchilla home. Doing so will ease your pet's transition to a new environment.

The cage bottom may be made of wire mesh or solid metal. Breeders prefer the wire bottom since this design enhances the cleanliness of the cage and the animal. It is also simple and inexpensive to maintain. The wire bottom supports the chinchilla, while openings in the mesh allow urine, droppings,

A solid cage bottom has no separation between the chinchilla and the litter. Two to 3 inches of litter line the bottom to absorb moisture and to provide a snug nest. The cage bottom is usually a removable pan which is pulled out like a drawer for cleaning. Unlike when using a cage with a wire bottom, the chinchilla must be removed during the cleaning. This type of cage must be cleaned more often since the chinchilla is in direct contact with soiled food and litter.

LOCATION: Deciding where to place the cage is an important consideration. Since chinchillas flourish in constant moderate temperatures, experts recommend indoor housing. A chinchilla kept outside, or in an uninsulated garage or attic, may become weak or ill due to the wide temperature fluctuations. Additionally, an escaped indoor pet can be easily captured; a chinchilla escaped from an outdoor enclosure will probably never be seen again.

Although native to South America, a mostly tropical continent, chinchillas actually thrive in cold, mountainous regions. For this reason, select a moderately cool location or one where the air circulates freely to avoid overheating. Temperatures above 80°F are uncomfortable for the chinchilla and may even be deadly. Don't place the cage in kitchens where drastic temperature changes are common or near heaters and radiators that are drying to the fur and skin. Protect the chinchilla from excessive smoke and humidity, and avoid areas of direct sunlight. Provide adequate ventilation but

A simple cardboard box makes a suitable toy for this chinchilla, but it will likely wind up being chewed.

Chinchillas need regular dust baths to keep their coats free of moisture and excess oil. They greatly enjoy this activity.

keep the cage away from drafty windows and doors. Chinchillas enjoy private burrows in the wild, and all-around exposure upsets them. Provide a feeling of security by placing the cage with one side against a wall. A corner is even better.

A simple cardboard box makes a wonderful retreat. Cut the flaps from the top, make a small door, and place the box upside down in the cage. A large juice can with both ends removed works well also. Smooth any sharp edges and flatten the bottom slightly to prevent rolling.

LITTER: Wood shavings are a perfect litter for the cage floor. They have a fresh scent and make a warm bed for a sleepy chinchilla. Shavings are also inexpensive and readily available at most pet shops. Some breeders use only softwood shavings, such as pine or spruce. Cedar shavings are popular and have a pleasant aroma. Do not use cedar, though, if your pet insists on chewing the litter as many chinchillas do. These chips contain a strong resin that can be harmful if consumed regularly. For this same reason, be sure no chips come from stained, glued, or lacquered wood. Your pet shop dealer will help you choose a clean, chemical-free shaving.

Fuller's earth is another good litter material. This clay-like substance is not as readily obtained as shavings, but it and products similar to it are commercially available at pet shops.

Some cat litters are made from ground clay similar to Fuller's earth. Choose a brand that has not been treated with chemicals or odor neutralizers.

Don't cut corners choosing cage litter, particularly for a solid bottom cage. Newspapers do not effectively absorb moisture, and the ink rubs off to stain the chinchilla's fur. Sawdust and sand scatter easily as your pet scampers in its cage. By the end of a day, the cage will be empty of litter and your floor will be a mess. Ground corn cobs are inexpensive and absorbent, but they may carry mites. Hay and straw become moldy if left in the cage too long, and when wet they stain your pet's fur.

FEED AND WATER HOLDERS: The cage must be equipped with the proper feed containers. A small pellet dish is required, preferably one that hangs on or is fastened to the side of the cage. These models give a constant supply of fresh food that cannot be soiled by droppings, and take up a minimum of space.

A ceramic dish with a heavy bottom to prevent tipping is also suitable. Slightly elevate the dish to keep out stray litter and to prevent the food from being soiled with urine.

A closed water system is a necessity for chinchillas because a water bowl is quickly polluted with droppings, urine, litter, and food. An inverted glass or plastic bottle attaches to the outside of the cage by a wire holder and a small metal tube extends into the cage. As the chinchilla laps at the end of the tube, fresh water is provided. Use only metal drinking tubes for chinchillas; glass tubes are bitten and chewed.

Holders are available for loose hay and hay cubes, but they are not necessary. Hay and hay cubes may be placed on the cage floor in small amounts if the litter is changed frequently. If hay holders are used, be sure the hay is within easy reach. Check that the cube holder grips the block firmly; the hay should not slide as the chinchilla tries to nibble.

MISCELLANEOUS SUPPLIES: Chinchillas are active animals and enjoy chewing best of all. Satisfy this craving by providing plenty of chew toys. A block of wood that is free of chemicals and insects provides hours of fun. A simple and inexpensive toy, the wood will be picked up, rolled around, and used as a perch and bed. The chewing activity also keeps the teeth in excellent condition.

Pumice may be purchased in small ready-to-use squares called "chew blocks", or chunks may be cut from a larger piece. A 4-inch square lasts a long time and is a fine chew toy.

Exercise wheels are an outlet for a chinchilla's abundant energy. Used mostly at night, a wheel keeps your pet fit and lively.

This photo clearly illustrates the thickness and texture of the chinchilla's fur. Garments made from chinchilla fur are very expensive.

Seeds and nuts are good treats for chinchillas. Just be sure to feed them in moderation.

An artificial heat source is soothing if your chinchilla is ill, sleepy, or the room is drafty. Low wattage heating pads are manufactured especially for chinchillas and provide the appropriate level of heat. They are firm, flat, and fit under a corner of the pan of a solid cage bottom. In a wire bottom cage the pad is held in place with springs. A thin piece of wood prevents the chinchilla from touching the pad yet allows the heat to come through. No matter which cage type you have, make sure that the pad and the cord are well out of the chinchilla's reach.

A heat lamp placed over a corner of the cage works just as well. A 15-watt incandescent bulb is best. Higher wattage bulbs produce heat that may be uncomfortable and may be fatal to young chinchillas. Consider placing the heat source near the chinchilla's cardboard box "hideout". It makes a cozy, warm sleeping area.

A piece of carpet is a nice luxury item for a chinchilla, especially if your pet is kept in a wire bottom enclosure. Remnants can be obtained at carpet stores for a reasonable price. The carpet will be used for sleeping and playing as it is flipped and dragged throughout the cage.

If there is room in the cage to keep a dust bath, keep it covered with a board when not in use. The closed bath substitutes as a perch or shelf. Reinforce the edges with a thin sheet of metal to deter chewing. A small wire affixed to the cover can be extended between the bars so that the bath may be opened and closed without reaching inside the cage.

SANITATION: Chinchillas are naturally clean animals. Keeping their cage tidy encourages grooming and promotes good health.

A few daily chores are required. Before feeding, remove any leftover food and hay from the cage and clean the feed containers. Pellets cannot be reused even if they appear untouched, because they may be contaminated with urine of droppings. Rinse and refill the water bottle with fresh liquid.

Once a week the tray bottom should be removed and washed. Ordinary soap and warm water works fine. Mild dishwashing liquids and liquid hand soaps dissolve easily. Scrub the inside of the water bottle with a stiff brush. It is not necessary to disinfect it with chlorine bleach if it is rinsed and cleaned regularly. Remove any loose fur clinging to the cage.

If your chinchilla is ill, follow the cleansing with a mild disinfectant, such as caustic soda. Chlorine bleach may be used if added sparingly to the water. Rinse the cage well and allow it to dry thoroughly before replacing the litter.

Twice yearly, just before and after winter, disinfect the cage and all the accessories, including the dust bath. Loosen debris with a stiff brush and allow the equipment to dry in the sun.

Your chinchilla will enjoy gnawing on Oodles™, manufactured by the Nylabone Corporation.

NUTRITION

A chinchilla's diet is uncomplicated, inexpensive, and readily available throughout the year. The staple foods are pellets, hay, and water. Supplements and treats are given at the discretion of the individual chinchilla fancier.

PELLETS: Commercial chinchilla pellets are a mixture of wheat germ, alfalfa meal, oats, molasses, soybean oil meal, corn, vitamins, and minerals. Unfortunately, most chinchilla pellets can be obtained only in bulk. Since they lose most of their nutritional value within 60 days, they are not a practical purchase for the average pet owner. (A chinchilla eats about two tablespoons of pellets a day.) Rabbit and guinea pig pellets are both acceptable substitutes, but the guinea pig pellets are fortified with hormones and have a higher

These bone-hard gnaw snacks are available at pet shops everywhere.

fat content. Therefore, a chinchilla may get too fat in a few months.

If your pet is in good condition when you bring it home, you'll want to continue using the same brand of pellets as the pet shop used. If this is not possible, ask the dealer for at least a week's supply of his feed and gradually mix in the new brand of pellets. Chinchillas are sensitive to dietary changes, and their digestive system must be given time to adjust.

HAY: Hay for chinchillas must not have been treated with chemicals and insecticides. It must never be too fresh and must be dried and cured carefully to prevent the development of mold. The hay must always be brittle enough to be crushed in your hand. If it loses its crispiness during humid weather, it must be re-dried. Spread the hay outdoors in the sun or set it in a cardboard box placed next to a radiator or stove.

Dry, pressed hay cubes or "mini-bales" are a common alternative. These cubes are pelleted blocks of chopped hay that retain their nutritional value for a long time if stored in a dry place. The hard surface is good for gnawing, and the solid block is rolled around for entertainment. A chinchilla should receive a handful of loose hay or one mini-bale each day.

WATER: An adult chinchilla drinks about a tablespoon of water every day. Fresh water must be available at all times.

FEEDING TIMES: Chinchillas should be fed and watered at the same time every day. Usually the bulk of the hay and pellets is given early in the evening when the animals become active. A smaller portion is offered in the morning.

Monitor your pet's intake and eating habits daily. Any change from the usual is often a sign of illness.

SUPPLEMENTS AND TREATS: Supplements are not necessary if you provide your chinchilla with a healthy diet. However, at times a chinchilla may need extra nutrition: during rapid growth stages, while pregnant or nursing, or when recovering from an illness. Commercial treats are available or they can be homemade. Formula consisting of equal parts of wheat germ, powdered milk, rolled oats, and baby cereal and equal parts of rolled oats and powdered milk are good mixes. Since supplements are rich, limit the servings to one a day to avoid too much weight gain.

Raisins, sunflower seeds, and peanuts are excellent treats in moderation. Chinchillas are also fond of the branches of fruit trees. Select only branches from trees that have seeds (pear, mulberry), not stones (cherry, plum), in the fruit. Be sure the branches have not been sprayed with insecticide. Offer treats sparingly or your chinchilla may refuse to eat its ration of pellets and hay. If you have several chinchillas, do not offer one a treat and ignore the others. These animals are sensitive to preferential treatment.

GROOMING AND TAMING

DUST BATHING

Chinchillas need regular baths to remove excess natural oils and moisture from their fur. They don't "bathe" in water but in finely ground sand, a dust similar to the volcanic ash found in the Andes. Special chinchilla dust is available in some pet shops. Sometimes it can only be obtained in bulk, but this is not a problem since it is inexpensive and lasts indefinitely. Do not substitute other powders even if they look and feel the same. An unsuitable dust can cause serious problems.

Put at least 2 inches of powder in a container large enough for a chinchilla to flip and roll around in. It should be deep enough to prevent too much of the powder from being tossed out. Metal bread pans, plastic bowls, and even large glass jars turned on their sides are all suitable. Just remember that the container has to be larger than the chinchilla but small enough to fit through the cage door.

Since chinchillas are nocturnal creatures, a good time to offer the bath is in the morning. It is, after all, because of their nighttime activity that a bath is both welcomed and needed. Allow the chinchilla to cavort in the bath for five or ten minutes. Only a few flips are needed to loosen and clean the fur.

Usually a bath every couple of days is all that is required. If you notice that the chinchilla's fur seems flat, separates easily, or feels damp to the touch, offer dust baths more often. In more humid

Offer your chinchilla a bath when the fur seems flat, separates easily, or feels damp to the touch. The chinchilla's antics in the "tub" are fun to watch.

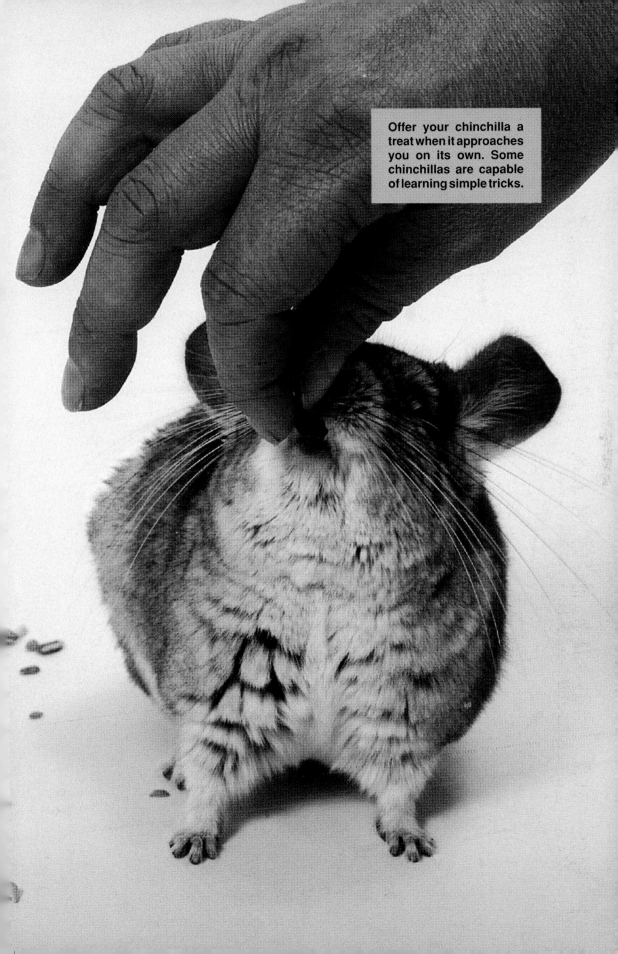

Offer your chinchilla a treat when it approaches you on its own. Some chinchillas are capable of learning simple tricks.

weather, a bath may be needed daily. However, if the chinchilla begins to scratch a lot, cut back on the baths. Too much bathing has resulted in dry skin.

The dust can be reused several times. After each bath, remove the powder that has become soiled by urine and replace it with fresh powder. Sift the sand weekly to remove any droppings. To prevent the spread of disease, every chinchilla should have its own bath.

Young chinchillas need to be introduced to the bath, or they may refuse to use it once they are weaned. Older chinchillas that have been denied a bath for several weeks may become accustomed to not having it and then can't be enticed to bathe again.

GROOMING

Combing improves a chinchilla's appearance by removing loose fur as the animal sheds. It also lessens the amount of hair that can float throughout the house.

Cover your lap with an old towel or cloth to catch the hair and protect your clothing. Steady the chinchilla on your lap by holding the base of its tail or supporting the animal under the chest with your hand. Starting at the rear, use a wide-toothed comb to lift and separate small sections of hair at a time. Work toward the neck until the back and sides are smooth. When finished, repeat the process with a fine-toothed comb. Grooming the belly fur is unnecessary.

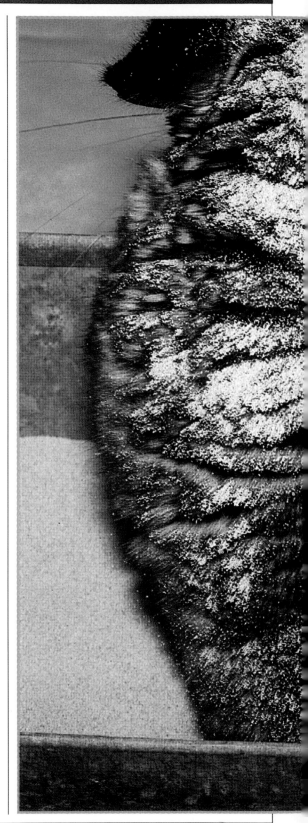

The dust that is used in the bath is similar to the volcanic ash found in the Andes, which is the native region of the chinchilla.

It is better to comb a chinchilla before a dust bath rather than after. Combing allows the dust to penetrate more deeply and clean more thoroughly.

SHEDDING

Chinchillas shed their hair naturally about every three months, so don't be alarmed if you notice more fur flying around at times. The new fur growth typically begins at the head and works its way down the back and sides. Sometimes just behind the new growth is a distinct line called the priming line. It distinguishes the old growth from the new. When the priming line reaches the tail, the chinchilla's fur is considered prime and in the best condition. In several weeks the growth process will begin again.

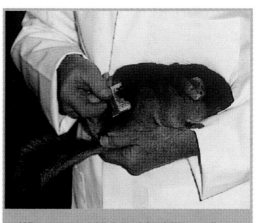

When grooming a chinchilla, a fine-toothed comb works best.

TAMING

Consider the chinchilla's age when you are trying to tame it. Youngsters under three weeks old are quite averse to being caught and fondled. If the mother is nearby and she is calm in your presence, the baby will eventually follow its mother's example. Do handle these young chinchillas, though, because the more familiar they are with humans the better pets they will make.

Chinchillas between six and eight weeks of age are eager to get out of the cage but will usually struggle to be free. The animal wants to explore everything in sight. After they're weaned, chinchillas settle down a bit and are much easier to handle.

The first step in taming any pet is to gain its trust. With gentle, consistent coaching from a serious trainer, a chinchilla will respond favorably in a short amount of time. A chinchilla can become tame, and some are even capable of learning a few simple tricks.

When taming, the room should be quiet and not full of people. The less extraneous activity in the room, the less distraction for the chinchilla.

Approach the cage slowly but deliberately, speaking softly to keep the animal calm. Initially, do not attempt to touch it; simply allow it to adjust to your approach. When you can come close to the chinchilla without creating a great deal of excitement, open the cage door. Place your hand inside without trying to touch or handle the chinchilla.

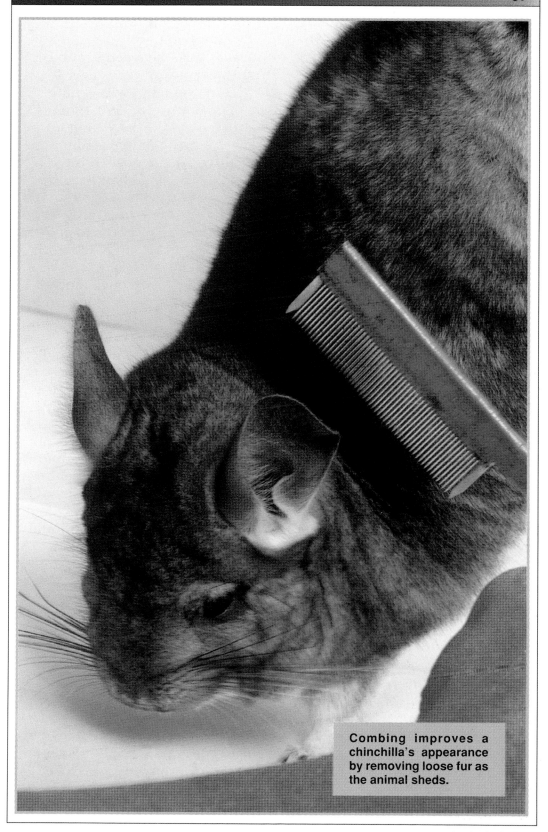

Combing improves a chinchilla's appearance by removing loose fur as the animal sheds.

At first the animal may scamper about, but soon its curiosity will cause it to sniff and explore this unfamiliar object. Try to scratch the chinchilla behind the ears or under the chin. Eventually it may sit in your hand and allow you to pick it up. Be persistent, but don't rush the animal. Each chinchilla has its own disposition and will respond in its own time.

the entire time looking for another morsel. Additionally, the scent of the food will linger on your fingers and the chinchilla may bite them.

As the animal becomes accustomed to your touch, you'll want to remove it from the cage. Don't be disappointed, though, when you realize that your pet is interested in more than just you. It will want to explore its

If a chinchilla feels cornered, it may bite. Approach the cage calmly, and let your pet sniff your hand before you try to pick it up.

Always end a taming session with plenty of praise and a treat such as a raisin or sunflower seed. Don't offer the tidbit at the beginning of the session because the chinchilla will probably spend

surroundings, and this means every nook and cranny. Therefore, "chinchilla-proof" a room before you let the animal roam. Check to see that the chinchilla can be easily retrieved from everything it

You'll know that your chinchilla is becoming tame when it readily eats from your hand.

can hide under or behind. Examine everything low to the ground to make sure that all small holes and crevices have been safely blocked. You'll find spaces you never knew existed. My chinchilla found a cozy spot underneath the bathroom sink. Once I finally enticed her out of there and sealed it up, she found one just as good under a kitchen cabinet!

Feeding a chinchilla only in its cage will train it to return there when hungry. Nothing is more effective in enticing a stubborn chinchilla to return to its cage than filling a dish with fresh food.

Simple tricks like responding to its own name can be learned by some chinchillas. Natural behaviors such as resting on its haunches will be performed on command if you provide the

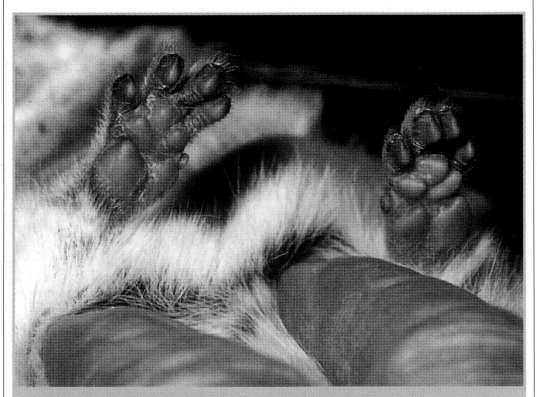

The undersides of a chinchilla's paws are amply padded.

Allowing a chinchilla to come out of the cage for exercise may promote better health. Always supervise your pet during its free time to prevent it from chewing furniture, plants, wallpaper, electrical cords, and the like. Provide it with plenty of chew toys for amusement.

proper reinforcement. As with taming, advanced training results from the use of positive reinforcement and lots of repetition. State a one-word command. When the chinchilla has given the desired response, reward it with a treat so that it relates the command, the act, and

A chinchilla's ears are large and prominent. The fur on them is not as thick as that on the rest of the body.

the reward. Do not confuse the chinchilla with too many things at once, and keep the tricks simple.

The least you should expect from a tame chinchilla is to have it rest comfortably on your hand without biting or fleeing. With the chinchilla feeling safe and secure in your hands, examination and treatment will be easier.

to squirm under thorny bushes and slip through the holes in some chain link fences. Furthermore, the outdoors is not an ideal environment in which to teach your friend new tricks.

SHOWS

Chinchilla shows are sponsored by local, state, and national

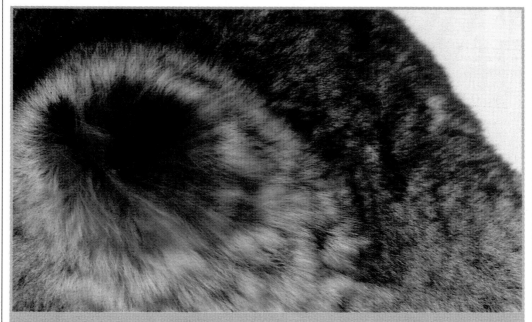

Blowing into the fur reveals the gradations of color on the hairs.

OUTDOOR EXCURSIONS

You may want to take your pet outside on a cool day. Protect the chinchilla against overheating and bring it indoors immediately if it starts to breathe heavily, the ears become flushed, or it wants to lie on its side.

If you take the chinchilla outdoors and let it out of the cage, select a well-confined area. A chinchilla may wander away. If frightened by strange noises, it will dash for cover. Bear in mind that a chinchilla is small enough

organizations. Some shows permit only members of particular clubs to compete while others allow anyone to enter. Almost all shows, though, are open to the public for viewing. A chinchilla show is not the place for a pet fancier to compete against the finest specimens that professional chinchilla ranchers have to offer, but it is a great opportunity to see some of the most outstanding chinchillas in the country and talk to some experienced breeders.

A healthy chinchilla will have a dry nose. Its eyes will show no evidence of weeping.

Standard gray chinchilla mother with young. Overcrowding the cage is to be avoided, as it can cause stress.

Competitions not only allow ranchers to "show off" their stock, they teach you to identify the traits that make a quality chinchilla. Both standards and mutations are shown at competitions. The showing system can be confusing, but once you understand the procedure you'll realize that it varies little from show to show. Pick up a classification sheet to help you follow the show's progress and to jot down notes. Don't be afraid to ask questions if you become confused.

Walk around and inspect the animals, but never move a cage or attempt to touch an entry. Stay around for the finals and see if the judges agree with your choice.

A pet-quality chinchilla can make as good a pet as can a show-quality specimen.

BREEDING

Starting a chinchilla family requires forethought and planning. Consider where the adults will be bred. Adult chinchillas are a bit fussy about their breeding environment, therefore they must feel secure in their surroundings. A quiet area with a minimum of traffic

Before breeding a prospective pair, they should be allowed to get used to each other and recognize each other's scent. This is simply a matter of putting their cages adjacent to each other. Do this for at least a week before putting them together.

affords an ideal spot. A busy or noisy location inhibits breeding. Natural predators, such as rats, and other animals, such as dogs and cats, should not have access to the breeding rooms.

Plans must be made for the young. Litters range from one to six kits, with two being the average. A separate cage is needed for weaning. If you intend to keep the young, each will require its own cage.

If you did not buy a heating pad or low wattage bulb before, one is essential now. The warmth comforts the expectant mother and prevents litter mortalities by protecting the young from exposure to the cold. The firstborn

may die without the added heat if the mother cannot attend to it while giving birth to the rest of the litter. The extra heat also helps to dry the mammary gland infections.

NEST BOXES

When the breeding room is not centrally heated, professional ranchers construct nest boxes that attach onto the mother's cage. The mother and kits exit and enter through a hole cut in the wire. The wooden nest box is not large, but it is roomy enough to provide a cozy area for the mother and her young. A heat source placed beneath a false bottom provides warmth. The electric cord extends out and away from the box, always beyond the chinchilla's reach.

Do not fashion a nest box from sheet metal. Although it is durable, the metal rusts easily and does not retain heat well. In the event of a power failure, the metal cools quickly. Water will condense on its interior and chill the young, possibly killing them.

CHOOSING A MATE

After you confirm the sex of your chinchilla, consider its age and experience. Chinchillas are best bred around eight months of age. At this age they are sexually mature, playful, and less likely to fight than are older animals.

INTRODUCING THE PAIR

Your chosen pair must be properly introduced. Chinchillas need time to get acquainted before they are housed together. Once comfortable, the couple can share the same cage during and after breeding.

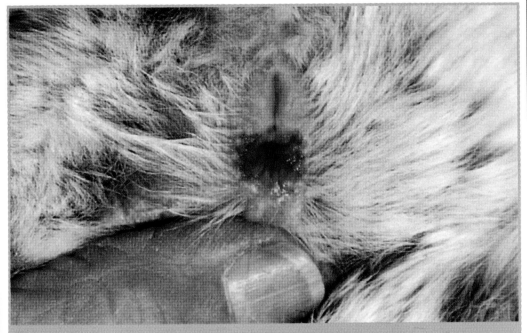

Genital region of a female chinchilla that is in full estrus after having delivered a litter.

Do not breed an older, experienced chinchilla to a younger one that has never been mated before. The result could be fatal. An experienced male is primarily concerned with mating and may become so impatient with a young female's playfulness that he will bite her severely. An experienced female may so aggressively reject and frighten an inexperienced male that he will never be capable of breeding. It is best to begin your chinchilla breeding with two young and inexperienced animals.

Initially, the animals are confined to their respective cages. The cages are placed next to one another for at least a week. During this time the chinchillas will sniff each other and become accustomed to each other's distinctive odor.

Next, gently place the male in the female's cage. Monitor their reactions carefully. You must be prepared to separate the animals if one violently rejects the other. Keep a pair of leather or garden gloves close by to protect your hands if you must intervene. You

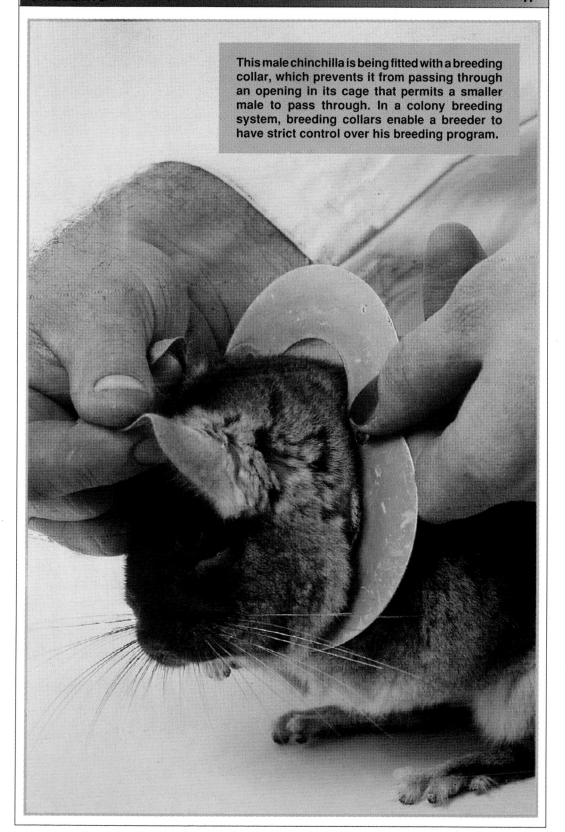

This male chinchilla is being fitted with a breeding collar, which prevents it from passing through an opening in its cage that permits a smaller male to pass through. In a colony breeding system, breeding collars enable a breeder to have strict control over his breeding program.

could also trap one of the animals in an overturned oatmeal container and remove it from the cage.

The male will probably spend the first few moments investigating his new surroundings before he acknowledges the female. The female, though, is totally concerned with the intruder in her home. As the male turns his attention to her, some roughhousing can be expected. The pair will chase each other around the cage and may nibble one another's fur and ears.

The rough and tumble antics are natural. Unless blood is drawn or one panics and attacks the other, do not separate the chinchillas. Fur will really begin to fly at this time. The female may also express her disfavor by retreating to a corner, rising on her haunches, and shooting urine at the male. If she does this, she is readying for a fight; remove the male at once.

Don't let a bad first encounter discourage you. Usually the chinchillas simply need a bit more time as neighbors. Another week side by side should lessen the friction and make them more receptive when they are reintroduced. It is rare for a chinchilla to adamantly refuse a mate. If this is the situation, replace the more aggressive partner.

MATING

After acceptance, mating occurs. The female becomes restless, alerting the male that she is physically ready to breed. The vagina, which is normally tightly closed, opens and becomes oval-shaped. This cycle (estrus or heat) is repeated about every 28-34 days. (In a young female, the vagina may be blocked by a rigid membrane, making penetration difficult. Apply a mild ointment or petroleum jelly for easier mating.) Some females may discharge a small, white waxy material, referred to as an "estrous" or "heat" plug, from the vagina.

The male senses the change in the female and courts her. Although a female is physically able to mate, she may be less than eager to do so. Remove any "hideouts" in the cage to prevent her retreat. After a slight scuffle, the male is usually successful. If he becomes too rough, remove him for a few hours until the female is ready to accept him. When she is, they may mate several times. Just because you haven't observed the coupling does not mean that mating has not occurred. The event may be quite brief or it may have taken place at night.

After mating, the male may make a short hiccupping sound. Another wax-like substance, the copulatory plug, may be found on the cage floor the next day. This plug aids fertilization by holding the semen in the vagina.

The male may remain with the female until the kits are born. He helps with the delivery by drying and warming the young.

MATING TROUBLES

If the chinchillas refuse to mate, consider changing their

surroundings. A different room or extra peace and quiet may do the trick.

Check the female for a vaginal infection if she has not conceived after several matings. Undetected infections may result in sterility. An unusual discharge may go

protective shaft. The penis dries and the area becomes quite painful. Apply petroleum jelly to moisten the penis and remove the hair. Gently maneuver the penis back into the sheath. Check him periodically for redness or swelling, which indicate infection.

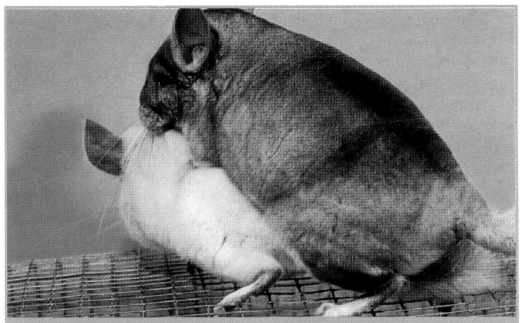

Chinchillas mating. Chinchillas may mate several times during a breeding session.

unnoticed if the female licks it as she cleans herself. Have a friend securely hold the chinchilla as you gently insert a cotton-tipped swab dipped in Panalog (an ointment available at your veterinarian) into her vagina. The swab should come out clean. A brown or red stain indicates an infection that should be treated by a veterinarian.

After several copulations, the male may develop a "hair ring" around his penis. The chinchilla is unable to remove this himself, and it prevents the penis from being withdrawn into the

If you can't pinpoint any problem yet no pregnancy results, consider the possibility that one or both of the chinchillas may be sterile.

PREPARING FOR THE LITTER

The litter will be born 111 days, give or take a day or two, after conception. Provide the female with extra hay and feed to accommodate her increased nutritional requirements. Some authorities suggest giving her commercial supplements to ensure a balanced diet. A homemade mix of equal parts of

In a harem breeding system, the male makes his way through the main passageway to visit the females that have been selected for breeding.

rolled oats, powdered milk, wheat germ, and baby cereal is fortifying.

About midway through the term, the female may have a loss of appetite and drop some weight. There is no cause for alarm unless other signs of disease are present.

This is a particularly stressful time for the chinchilla, so provide a relaxing environment and do not handle her at all. Any strain or handling may injure the fetuses and cause the female to resorb or abort them. Therefore, resist the urge to check the mother's growing tummy and certainly don't remove her from her familiar surroundings.

BIRTH

A few days before the litter is due, the mother may lose her appetite, drink more water, and have soft droppings. She may be less active, lying around and stretching more. A dust bath is not given at this time, since she may contract a vaginal infection.

Birth typically occurs during the early morning hours. Although she usually requires no assistance, you should be available in case of an emergency. She may have a difficult delivery or she may need help caring for the newborn. Make sure the cage remains warm.

During labor, the chinchilla is obviously uncomfortable. She may stretch up, perspire, and cry audibly. The fluid in the sac surrounding the kits is released and the contractions are visible. The babies should appear in two to three hours. The mother gently pulls a kit out with her teeth, removes the sac from the kit, then cleans and dries the baby's fur. When the afterbirth arrives, the birth process is over. The mother normally eats the afterbirth (for hormones to produce milk), but some breeders prefer to remove it. If labor lasts over four hours, or if the contractions stop before the kits arrive, call the vet immediately.

Should the mother be unable to care for the firstborn while more kits are emerging, and the father makes no attempt to warm them, the kit may become rigid from the cold. Remove the baby from the cage and warm it slowly in your gently clasped hands. Exhale short, easy breaths close to its mouth to encourage respiration. You can also try submerging the kit in warm water up to its neck.

The science of chinchilla breeding is a complex subject that requires extensive research if a breeding program is to be successful.

It may take up to 15 minutes until you see a response from the kit, but keep up the effort. When the baby is able to stand, dry it gently and return it to its mother.

CARE OF THE MOTHER

The new mother will be understandably weak after giving birth. She must eat well to properly care for her kits. If her appetite declines or she does not produce enough milk for nursing, add some apple vinegar to her drinking water. The vinegar sparks her appetite and helps her to regain weight. Authorities recommend about half a teaspoon per 250 ml. (about half a pint—one cup) of water. Change the water daily and discontinue the vinegar when she is eating well.

Chinchilla litters can range from one to four in size, but two is the average.

Chinchillas are weaned at the age of about six to eight weeks.

Illustration of the physical development of a chinchilla from conception to adult specimen.

The female needs time to be in top breeding condition again. Since she can conceive shortly after birth, remove the male when all the young have been delivered. Do not reintroduce him until the kits have been weaned.

REARING NEWBORNS

Kits look for their first meal within one hour of birth. The mother feeds them from a standing position, unlike cats and dogs, which lie on their sides. If the young fight over the teats, check the mother for bites and apply a mild ointment. If they continue fussing, ask your vet to clip their teeth to protect the mother. Nursing is difficult for a mother with swollen, inflamed teats. Apply camphor oil to each nipple to restore the free flow of milk.

A well-nourished female should have no problem supplying up to three kits with adequate milk. Since most litters consist of only two young, lack of milk is usually not a problem. If there are more than three young, select the strongest kits and feed them from an eyedropper or small doll's bottle. Leave the smaller kits to nurse with the mother. Prepare a formula of one part milk powder, or sweetened condensed milk, with two parts lukewarm spring water. Whole milk mixed equally with spring water also works well. Do not boil the water and do not use water from a tap. The chlorine in the tap water is toxic to the kits.

To hand-feed a kit, hold it upright and dab a little formula on its lower lip. The baby may be confused and will need some time to learn what is expected. Eventually, the kit licks its lip and swallows the milk with a chewing motion. Never force the liquid into the kit's mouth—the milk may enter the lungs and kill it.

Kits eat small amounts at each feeding and must be fed often. The first week they must be fed every three or four hours. Gradually reduce the feedings to three times a day. Stop the meal when the kit turns its head from the dropper and licks its lips. A mere dropper or two is a sufficient feeding. If you cannot be home for all the feedings, put a small amount of formula in a bottle and hang it on the side of the cage. Be sure it is within reach of the kits. Gradually introduce solid food into the kits' diet.

WEANING

When the kits are six to eight weeks old, they must be separated from their mother and placed in another cage. Keeping the kits together at this time eases the stress of leaving their mother. If the female still has milk, return the young to her once or twice a day for a meal. Within two weeks, the kits should be content on their own and each must be given its own cage.

It is very important that you do not overfeed the young at this time; overfeeding kills adolescent chinchillas. Give them half the adult ration of pellets and hay. When they are five to six months old, slowly increase the rations to a full adult portion.

Chinchillas are considered fully
grown at the age of eight months.

HEALTH

Under the right conditions, chinchillas are hardy animals that will thrive in captivity. A clean cage and a proper diet are the most important aspects of preventive maintenance, making illness unlikely. Additionally, diseases have a less devastating effect on a well-maintained chinchilla. Accidents and illnesses can happen, but do not panic. For simple matters, refer to this book and others, your local pet shop salesperson, or a veterinarian. The earlier an ailment is detected, the easier it is to correct. Do not delay in calling a vet about more serious problems. Allowed to continue unchecked, a simple illness can develop into something more troublesome and even fatal.

There are some obvious signs of poor health. Note any changes in your chinchilla's disposition such as lethargy or loss of appetite. Changes in the color, consistency, or size of the droppings denote sickness. Droppings of a healthy chinchilla are plump, oval to rounded, slightly moist, and of a uniform size. The color varies from olive green to dark brown. Loss of balance or unsteadiness, any discharge from the eyes, nose, or mouth, and difficulty breathing are all warning signs that things are not well.

Never attempt to diagnose and treat a health problem on your own. Only your vet should do this.

Isolate chinchillas with infectious diseases away from all others. To prevent the disease from spreading, do not reintroduce the sick animals to the others until the crisis is over. Clean the cage and all the accessories, including the dust bath, with a disinfectant solution. Rinse and dry this equipment thoroughly before replacing the chinchilla.

ELEVATED TEMPERATURE

The simplest way to determine if your chinchilla has a temperature is to look at its ears. If they are warm to the touch and bright pink or red, the chinchilla's temperature is probably elevated.

EYE INFECTIONS

If the chinchilla's dull, "weepy" eyes are accompanied by red and swollen lids or a white discharge around the rim, it has an eye infection. Small pieces of dust or litter may have lodged in or scratched the eye, or lowered resistance due to stress or improper diet may have caused it. Adjust the diet accordingly and take the animal to a vet. The doctor will probably give you a prescription for an ophthalmic ointment. He will show you how to clean and medicate the eye. The condition will clear up in three or four days. During this time do not provide a dust bath.

COLDS

Dull, watery eyes without other signs of infection may indicate a cold or pneumonia. If the animal is listless and has an elevated temperature, monitor its breathing. Wheezing and difficulty breathing are signs of a stuffy head.

Treating a cold requires keeping the chinchilla warm and providing plenty of water. Complications indicating pneumonia should be checked by a vet. Do not dust bathe a chinchilla suffering from respiratory problems.

CONSTIPATION

Most commonly the result of an improper diet or a change in the diet, constipation is usually a temporary, controllable condition. The droppings are small, hard, and dry. Adjust the diet and give plenty of drinking water. (Water consumption is essential in helping to relieve constipation). Getting the chinchilla to exercise may also help to alleviate the problem. One trick is to offer a dust bath several times a day and allow the animal to "splash" about for as long as it wants.

A healthy chinchilla will have a dry nose with no evidence of discharge.

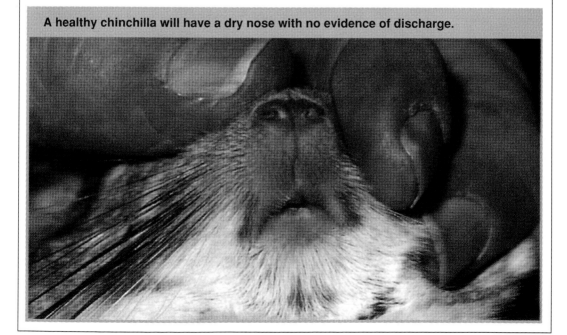

Check your pet's teeth regularly to see that they are worn down to the proper length. The yellowish cast to this chinchilla's teeth is normal for these animals.

DIARRHEA

Discolored or watery droppings signify diarrhea. The two main causes are overfeeding in juveniles and an improper or contaminated diet in adults.

Correct the diet and be vigilant in removing old and spoiled food from the cage. A little oxytetracycline may be added to the drinking water if the diarrhea is persistent.

Don't be overly concerned if soft but normally shaped droppings are seen in males prior to copulation and in females shortly after giving birth.

ENTERITIS

If your pet's diarrhea worsens and the droppings are coated with mucus and stuck together in long strings or surrounded by a jelly-like substance with air bubbles, it may be suffering from enteritis. The chinchilla may refuse to eat or may lose its balance when it tries to walk. Seek prompt medical attention by bringing the animal, along with a sample of the droppings, to the veterinarian. Enteritis may be caused by various forms of bacteria, and the vet needs to perform a microscopic examination of the droppings in order to prescribe the proper medication.

CUTS

Due to their protected environment and dense fur, bruises and cuts rarely occur in chinchillas. However, should one happen, simply cleanse the cut and in time it will heal. A light coating of antibiotic ointment can be applied, but take care not to smear it on the rest of the coat.

FUNGUS

Fungal infections occur most often during hot, humid weather, but they can appear at any time. The fur thins or falls out in patches, revealing red, irritated flesh. The infection is more easily seen around the moist areas of the body, such as the eyes, snout, and genitals.

Using a veterinary fungicide recommended by a veterinarian, dust the affected areas directly or add the medicine to the chinchilla's bath. The skin irritation should disappear in a few days, and new fur growth will be seen in a week. During muggy weather, the fungicide can be added regularly to the dust bath as a preventive measure.

the most popular theories involve a genetic factor, a protein-poor diet, and stress due to improper housing and handling. Presently there is no universal cure. Although fur chewing is not life-threatening, it certainly is unsightly.

If damaged fur has a wet, matted, or raggedly cut look, the chinchilla has probably been chewing on it. Check the diet and try to alleviate any stressful environmental conditions.

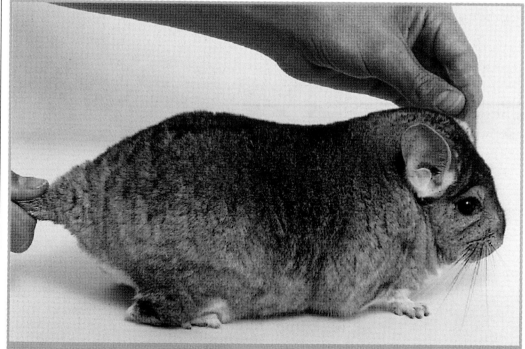
Regularly check your chinchilla for any abnormalities on its body.

If a fungal infection appears in one animal, all of your chinchillas must be treated. The disease is likely to have spread during the three-week incubation period of the fungus.

FUR BITING

No one is sure what causes fur biting (also called fur chewing), but

EAR PROBLEMS

Pawing at the ear, repeated tipping of the head to one side, walking around in circles, and drainage from the ear are all signs of an ear infection. A veterinarian will normally clean the ear and prescribe ear drops. Don't dust-bathe the chinchilla until it is off the medication.

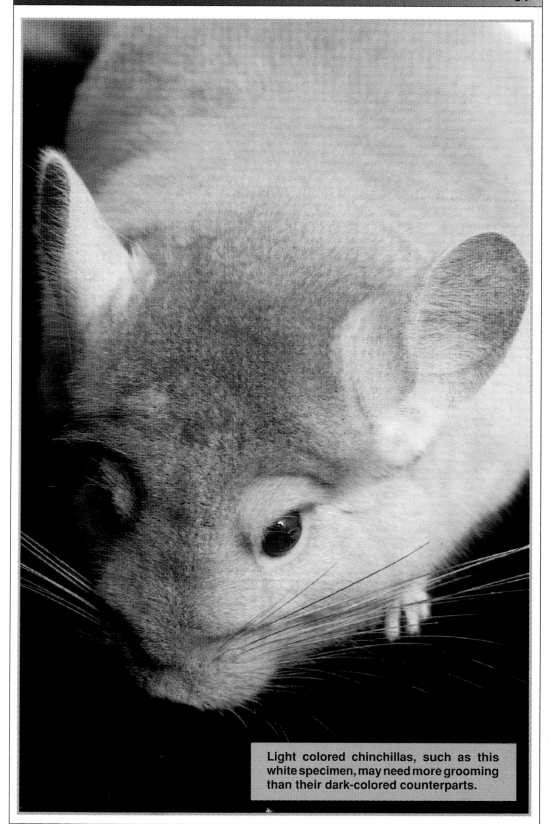

Light colored chinchillas, such as this white specimen, may need more grooming than their dark-colored counterparts.

Good husbandry—proper diet, clean cage, and regular grooming—is a very important element in your chinchilla's overall state of health.

Ear problems typically occur in conjunction with another infection or are the result of decreased resistance due to a poor diet.

MEDICATION

Don't use medicines that are diluted in the drinking water or sprinkled over the food. They may be easier to dispense than drops or pills, but they certainly won't be as reliable. Administering the medicine yourself is the only way

down the chinchilla's throat or you may cause it to choke.

VACCINATIONS

Chinchillas are such a hardy lot that vaccinations are not often recommended. However, there is a preventive vaccine to guard chinchillas against the most dangerous diseases. This is dispensed in two shots seven days apart, supplemented by an annual booster. More information can be obtained from your vet.

Chinchillas are dexterous little creatures. This chin is helping himself to a treat of fresh apple.

to be sure that your pet is getting the proper dose.

Hide a pill in a raisin or crush it up and roll the raisin in it. Use an eyedropper to dab liquid medicines on the chinchilla's lower lip. Apply drop after drop until all the medicine has been licked up. Never force the liquid

DISINFECTION

Whether a chinchilla dies of a disease or from an unknown cause, the cage and accessories need to be thoroughly disinfected before introducing another animal. Rinse all items and allow them to dry in the sun.